THE GOLDEN YEARS

text: David Sandison, Arthur Davis

design: Paul Kurzeja

SIENA

Welcome to *The Golden Years,* and to the first year in a new decade which really would go down in history as both remarkable and memorable. To some, the 1960s were memorable for an explosion of new and exciting musical and artistic talent - and so became the Swinging Sixties. To others, the decade would offer immense political upheaval and remarkable change. In this year of 1960, the young John Kennedy announced that he intended to become the Democratic Party's nominee in the forthcoming US presidential elections, and ended the year as his nation's youngest leader; the South African regime showed its true colours when it massacred 56 people in Sharpeville; the newly-independent Congo exploded into violence and bloodshed; a British court decided that *Lady Chatterley's Lover* was suitable reading for wives and servants; Nikita Khrushchev threatened to bury the West and outraged the United Nations when he took off a shoe to make his point; and General de Gaulle learned that there were people in the world more stubborn than he could ever be.

A young American boxer called Cassius Clay hit the world stage for the first time when he won an Olympic gold medal in the heat of a Roman summer, while his gifted compatriot, Wilma Rudolph, overcame that heat to win three golds of her own on the track.

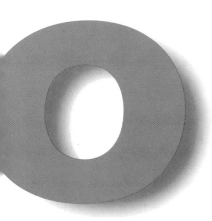

The movie world lost heart-throb Clark Gable, US pilot Gary Powers lost his freedom when the Russians shot down his U-2 spy plane, French literature lost a powerful voice with the passing of existentialist Albert Camus, and Britain's Labour Party lost one of its giants with the death of Nye Bevan.

A British princess married a commoner, France and Britain decided to unite in building the world's first supersonic passenger plane, and a 58-year-old cancer victim decided to defy the disease - and his doctors - by sailing the Atlantic single-handed.

It's all in here, and a lot more besides - the voices, the faces, the places and quite a few things you'd probably forgotten. Enjoy!

JANUARY 31

Kennedy To Run For US Presidency

JOHN FITZGERALD KENNEDY, Senator for the State of Massachusetts, today confirmed that he intended to be the Democratic Party candidate for the US Presidency in elections to be held at the end of the year. He would be assisted by his brother, Robert, who would mastermind a campaign which boasted offices all over the United States.

JFK's main Democratic rival was almost certain to be Minnesota's Senator Hubert Humphrey, but Kennedy's film-star looks, allied to his family's political heritage - his father, Joseph Kennedy, was the US Ambassador to Britain during the Second World War - had already given him an early clear advantage in opinion polls.

The young Kennedy's dream of running America came to him in 1955, when he was in hospital recovering from operations on his spine. The US electorate can have no reason to call him spineless, however. The operations were the legacy of injuries he sustained serving in the US Navy. A candidate for the Democratic Party's vice-presidential nomination in 1956, he lost out when Senator Estes Kefauver was preferred as Adlai Stevenson's electoral running mate.

His failure in that contest was generally believed to have been due to a combination of his youth - he was not yet 40 years old at the time - and the fact that he was a Roman Catholic. While he obviously remained a Catholic, his relative youth was now seen as an advantage

with an electorate believed to be looking for a change from the old guard.

Should Kennedy win the Democratic nomination, his opponent in the fight to replace President Dwight Eisenhower, who has to retire after two terms in office, will undoubtedly be Richard Nixon, who made history in 1952 by becoming the youngest ever Vice-President when he was Eisenhower's successful running mate.

Nasser Lays Aswan Foundations

In a ceremony full of triumph and hope, Egyptian President Gamal Nasser today laid the foundation-stone of the Aswan Dam - the world's biggest hydroelectric power complex - which is designed to transform Egypt's future by supplying enough energy to enable his dream of a modern industrial State to be realized.

It was one of Nasser's principal objectives to haul Egypt out of the morass of inefficiency and corruption he'd inherited in 1954 when he and a group of young military officers ousted King Farouk. If Egypt was to be a true leading player in the Middle East, it needed to be modernized. With Soviet help, he seemed about to ensure that status would be supported by all the power his people could use.

Africans Boycott Kenyan Talks

Everything was in place today in London: conference rooms, communications facilities for delegates, a press-room for journalists covering what was in every respect a historic series of meetings, and a team of British officials led by Colonial Secretary Iain Macleod, ready to talk.

There was only one snag. The people whom all this had been set up for didn't arrive.

The conference would get going in a few days, but for now the African delegates who should have been negotiating the constitution of a soon-to-be-independent Kenya were boycotting the event in protest at the initial terms set by the British Government.

Khrushchev Promises To Cut Troops

Wanting to show the world his conciliatory face only weeks before hosting a summit of world Communist Party leaders in Moscow, Soviet Premier Nikita Khrushchev today announced that he intended to reduce the USSR's armed forces over the next two years. The figure quoted by Khrushchev was 1.2 million, a target dismissed by Kremlin-watchers as pure propaganda. With the world no more stable than it had been in recent years, such a reduction was unthinkable. But it did make Comrade Chairman look like a man of peace and a true statesman.

UK TOP 10 SINGLES

1: What Do You Want To Make Those Eyes At Me For
- Emile Ford & The Checkmates

2: What Do You Want
- Adam Faith

3: Oh! Carol
- Neil Sedaka

4: Staccato's Theme
- Elmer Bernstein

5: Seven Little Girls Sitting In The Back Row
- The Avons

6: Little White Bull
- Tommy Steele

7: Starry Eyed
- Michael Holliday

8: Rawhide
- Frankie Laine

9: Why
- Anthony Newley

10: Way Down Yonder In New Orleans
- Freddy Cannon

ARRIVALS
Born this month

4: Michael Stipe, US rock musician, songwriter (REM)
11: Vicky Peterson, US rock musician, singer (The Bangles)
16: Sade Adu (Helen Folasade Adu), UK singer, songwriter
17: John Crawford, rock musician (Berlin)
27: Michael Hutchence, Australian rock singer, writer, actor (INXS)

JANUARY 29

Civil War Looms In Algeria

PRESIDENT CHARLES DE GAULLE donned his mothballed general's uniform tonight to broadcast a TV appeal ordering his army to break the French settler insurrection in Algeria, which he described as 'a foul blow against France'.

As tension grew in the North African province, it was unclear whether army officers would order troops to battle with heavily armed militia who'd occupied fortified positions near the University of Algiers. There is a fear that Frenchman will be seen to kill Frenchman, or that troops will refuse to fight.

So far, the main French casualties have been killed in sporadic clashes with police, paratroops or other line regiments recalled from action against Muslim nationalists. But de Gaulle's dismissal of General Jacques Massu, the Central Algiers Region military commander, on January 21 had created a crisis of confidence and duty. Massu's criticism of de Gaulle's offer of Algerian self-determination only echoed the feelings of many now being ordered to shoot compatriots.

JANUARY 27

BBC TV Plans A Second Channel

British TV bosses obviously didn't regard the viewing limitations imposed on Catholics this month (see separate story) as too significant - today, the BBC announced plans for a second channel of its own.

The BBC's understandable wish to regain the advantage it had before the arrival of ITV, prompted many to recall that, on the day of ITV's launch, in September 1955, the BBC purposefully started its evening transmissions 30 minutes earlier than its young rival's initial opening and - just to make sure that the young pretender had plenty of competition - the scriptwriters of the popular radio soap, The Archers ('an everyday story of country folk'), killed off leading character Grace Archer in a fire!

Catholics Warned Against Watching 'Unsafe' TV

Television is clearly a mixed blessing, but even so it was making huge strides in popularity in Britain. A survey conducted by the BBC and published this month concluded that half the country's population was watching the box at peak times. Perhaps this broad appeal was the reason why television came in for mention in new regulations laid down today at the first synod of the Roman Catholic Church ever held in Rome, in which increased austerity appeared to be the keyword. Once approved by Pope John XXIII, stricter rules relating to a variety of topics were expected to be adopted in dioceses all over the world. Apart from banning women with bare arms or wearing 'men's clothing' from receiving the sacraments, Roman Catholics will be only permitted to watch films and TV programmes considered 'safe' by the Vatican. Even more repressive regulations are to be applied to the clergy - priests will not be allowed to enjoy tobacco in public, nor can they visit either cinemas or theatres.

Literary World Mourns Shute And Camus

The first month of the new decade brought the unrelated deaths of two acclaimed but very different novelists, Nevil Shute and Albert Camus.

Shute (real name Nevil Shute Norway), was famous for such best-sellers as *A Town Like Alice* - the story of a soldier's redemption in the remote Australian settlement of Alice Springs after he'd undergone torture during the Second World War - and *On The Beach*, the thought-provoking tale of the victims of a fortunately fictional Third World War. Both also became the basis of successful movies. Shute died on January 12, only days before his 61st birthday.

Albert Camus, the French author considered by many to be on a par with Jean-Paul Sartre in philosophical and intellectual terms, died in a car accident on January 4, at the age of 46. Born in Algeria, Camus was raised in poverty as the son of a domestic servant.

His most famous work was *The Outsider*, which concerned a murder committed by a man who could no longer stand the unreasonable tribulations of life which his intellect refused to accept. A one-time communist, Camus himself became very much an 'outsider', choosing to channel his distaste with much of modern society into the art of influential novels like *The Plague* and *The Fall*.

Both will be long remembered, although for very different reasons.

South Africans Seethe At Mac's 'Wind Of Change' Speech

'We may sometimes be tempted to say to each other, "Mind your own business." But in these days I would expand the old saying so that it runs, "Mind your own business, but mind how it affects mine, too".'

Urging South Africa's white rulers to move towards the policies of racial equality which Britain wanted to achieve throughout the British Commonwealth, Macmillan made it clear that he believed

WHITE SOUTH AFRICANS were in a rage today as British Prime Minister Harold Macmillan told a packed parliament in Cape Town: 'The wind of change is blowing through this continent and, whether we like it or not, this growth of national consciousness is a political fact.'

This smacked too much of meddling in their affairs for many local politicians, despite the Prime Minister adding,

the great issue was whether the 'uncommitted' peoples of Asia and Africa chose to swing towards the Communist East, or to the West.

The white parliament made its position clear, and its view of Macmillan's unwanted predictions, when it applauded premier Verwoerd's retort: 'There has to be justice not only for the black man in Africa, but also for the white man.'

Chinese Stay Away From Khrushchev's Party

The depths of the split between Soviet leader Nikita Khrushchev and Chinese supremo Mao Tse-tung became clear to the world today when no delegates from China turned up for the opening of the summit Khrushchev had called to show Communist Party solidarity.

Observers noted that the Chinese absence spelled the end of any pretence that the USSR and China were divided only by fine points of communist doctrine. Mao remained a staunch believer in the kind of autocratic control and fundamentalism of Josef Stalin, and considered Khrushchev's relative liberalism to be a complete betrayal of communist ideals.

De Gaulle Wins Emergency Powers

With the Algerian crisis worsening by the day, President Charles de Gaulle today won the year of emergency powers he'd demanded as the only way he could hope to tackle the ever-shifting tide of events, when the French National Assembly voted him the complete authority he'd wanted.

On February 10, de Gaulle confirmed the stance which had sparked the French settler revolt in January when he announced a new mandate for the North African province. Guaranteed to enrage the settlers even more, it spelled out his plan to give Algerian Muslims a better deal and a greater say in an eventually independent country.

Castro Jails Opponents, Grabs Industries

Fidel Castro, the President of Cuba since his guerrilla forces overthrew the regime of Fulgencio Batistá last January, increased his control of the island nation today when a Havana court sentenced 104 government opponents to varying lengths of time in prison, so clearing the way for his government to begin turning Cuba into the socialist State of his dreams.

Castro would make his most emphatic move on February 21 by announcing the nationalization of all private businesses - from companies once owned by US corporations, to corner shops selling tobacco and groceries. Everyone, it seemed, was going to be part of the adventure.

UK TOP 10 SINGLES

1: Why
- Anthony Newley
2: Voice In The Wilderness
- Cliff Richard
3: Way Down Yonder In New Orleans
- Freddy Cannon
4: Poor Me
- Adam Faith
5: Starry Eyed
- Michael Holliday
6: Pretty Blues Eyes
- Craig Douglas
7: On A Slow Boat To China
- Emile Ford & The Checkmates
8: What Do You Want To Make Those Eyes At Me For
- Emile Ford & The Checkmates
9: Beyond The Sea (La Mer)
- Bobby Darin
10: Heartaches By The Number
- Guy Mitchell

FEBRUARY 26

Princess Margaret To Marry Commoner

CELEBRATIONS WERE IN ORDER at Buckingham Palace today when Princess Margaret, the Queen's sister, announced her engagement to photographer Antony Armstrong-Jones. Although her fiancé was the son of the Countess of Rosse, and by definition a member of the nobility, under the terms of royal family qualifications he was a commoner.

Public reaction to the announcement included a degree of relief that the princess had finally found Mr Right. Memories were still fresh concerning her disastrous relationship with Group Captain Peter Townsend, a former equerry of the Duke of Edinburgh, whose divorced status far outweighed his standing as a war hero.

In 1955, Princess Margaret had succumbed to royal family and public pressure and ended her liaison with Townsend. Today's announcement seemed to signal a 'Happy ever after' conclusion.

It was, in fact, quite a month for the Buckingham Palace champagne stocks. On February 19, the Queen had given birth to her third child - and second son. He was to be called Andrew Albert Christian Edward.

In the last weeks of her pregnancy the Queen had found time to make a change in her family's future history, and on February 8 proclaimed that all her descendants not styled Royal Highness (which wouldn't include the new Prince Andrew) would henceforth be called by the new family name, Mountbatten-Windsor. It was her way of acknowledging the contribution she believed her uncle, Lord Louis Mountbatten, had made to Britain's recent past, and to whose family her husband, Prince Philip, belonged.

More Scrolls Found In Desert

Israeli archaeologists today claimed the most spectacular find of ancient biblical documents since the 1947 discovery of the so-called Dead Sea Scrolls. Like their predecessors, the new find is believed to have been hidden in caves by Hebrew bands who fled from the Roman occupation of Palestine some 1,700 years ago.

The scrolls, said to contain 'at least 16 verses from Exodus', were reported to be in excellent condition, if a little frayed. Preserved in the dry desert atmosphere, they were covered by nearly a foot of earth. Dating was achieved thanks to a coin found with them. It featured the head of the Emperor Trajan, who died in AD 117.

Bomb Blast Rocks American South

The tense deadlock which characterized much of the American South, as white power extremists continued to resist the breakdown of racial segregation, threatened to explode once more today when the home of a black student recently allowed to attend the Central High School in Little Rock, Arkansas, was the target for a bomb attack.

Only eight days later, the black civil rights leader, the Rev. Dr Martin Luther King, was arrested for perjury relating to his 1956 income tax return, an event which did little to calm the growing mood of unrest the Little Rock bomb had created.

It was a mood which would continue to simmer and occasionally boil over into riots, murder and civil disturbances throughout the new decade.

Britain To Fund Supersonic Passenger Plane

The shape of things to come - at least in the area of international travel - was unveiled today when the British Government announced that it had agreed to fund a supersonic airliner which could fly at 2,000 mph and reduce the flying time between, say, London and New York to a mere two hours.

The new aircraft could be built in partnership with the United States or France, according to Aviation Minister Duncan Sandys, but a number of leading British companies, including Vickers-Bristol-English Electric and Rolls-Royce, had been asked to study and solve certain problems.

Development costs were said to be high, with each aircraft reckoned to cost 'between £5 million and £6 million' ($12m and $15m).

MAR

Elvis Returns To Claim His Rock Crown

A HOWLING BLIZZARD, 2,000 screaming fans, and Frank Sinatra's daughter, Nancy, greeted Elvis Presley today at McGuire Airbase, New Jersey, when a US Army transport plane, which had brought him back from two years' exile in Germany as an ordinary serviceman, touched down.

Within two days, the man considered as the King of Rock 'n' Roll was discharged from the US Army, and returned to the career which made him an overnight sensation in the second half of the 1950s, both as a recording artist and budding film star.

The presence of Nancy Sinatra at Presley's return seemed to confirm the star's denials that there was anything in his relationship with Priscilla Beaulieu, the 16-year-old daughter of a US officer he was known to have dated in Germany, especially when it was announced that his first post-army TV appearance would be as special guest on *The Frank Sinatra Timex Show.*

Before that was transmitted on March 26, Presley had undertaken two days of recording in Nashville, and his new single, *Stuck On You,* was in the shops only 48 hours after the studio sessions. *Stuck On You* and its B-side, *Fame And Fortune,* were two of the songs he performed on the televised summit meeting of two giants of popular music, while he also sang with Sinatra. Elvis was back !

MARCH 11

Lumumba Emerges As New Congo Voice

Patrice Lumumba, the former postal clerk who had risen to a position of power as founder of the Congolese National Movement - the nationalist group demanding independence from Belgium since 1958 - was finally given the national platform he and his followers had been denied when he was allowed to address a public meeting in the Congolese capital, Léopoldville, today.

Riot police stood waiting in case of trouble, but while the meeting itself went off peacefully, Lumumba's speech inspired large numbers of other black citizens to riot in support of his message. The next day, Belgian authorities declared martial law to enable them to subdue the violence, in which 14 people were reported killed.

MARCH 14

Israel And Germany In Historic Talks

A memorable and historic day in New York saw the first meeting between the leaders of Israel and West Germany. Prime Minister David Ben-Gurion and Chancellor Konrad Adenauer were said to have had friendly talks, but had avoided the major - and still sensitive - issue of renewing full diplomatic relations.

Chancellor Adenauer said that he was delighted that reparations from West Germany were helping Israel, a nation whose citizens West Germany had long admitted were owed a huge debt of honour for their treatment during WWII.

For his part, Ben-Gurion said: 'The Germany of today is not the Germany of yesterday. We remember the past, not in order to brood upon it, but in order that it shall never recur.'

MARCH 1

Agadir Smashed As Quake Hits Morocco

The resort of Agadir was reported to have been completely destroyed today as the coast of Morocco was hit by a massive earthquake, then by a tidal wave, and finally by widespread fires which swept through the city. More than 1,000 people - some of them European tourists - were said to have been killed.

One of the first to reach the destruction was Morocco's Crown Prince Moulay Hassan, who directed and took part in rescue work among the ruins. Part of that rescue saw 50 ambulance planes flying some of the thousands of injured out of the area.

Vowing to rebuild Agadir, Hassan said, 'The old one has ceased to exist.' Reporters who managed to get into Agadir, which had a warning tremor the evening before, said that nothing higher than two-storey buildings remained intact.

ARRIVALS
Born this month:
7: Ivan Lendl, Czech tennis superstar
8: Peter 'Pedro' Gill, UK pop musician (Frankie Goes To Hollywood)
13: Adam Clayton, Irish rock musician (U2)
21: Ayrton Senna, Brazilian Formula One racing star
25: Steve Norman, UK pop musician (Spandau Ballet)

MARCH 21

World Stunned As SA Police Kill 56 In Sharpeville

WORLD OPINION, already largely ranged against the apartheid regime in South Africa, was given fresh reason for outrage today. Sharpeville, a black township in the Transvaal, was the scene of a massacre when police opened fire on a crowd of 15,000 people surrounding the local police station as part of a campaign of civil disobedience against so-called 'pass laws' which obliged black Africans to carry identity cards at all times and limited their freedom to live and work where they wanted.

What had been intended as a peaceful protest spilled over into a full-blown battle when stones were thrown at a line of armed policemen who opened fire on the advancing protesters, killing 56 people and wounding 162 others.

As ambulances raced back and forth from what one eyewitness described as 'a world war battlefield, with bodies sprawled all around', a local hospital was forced to put some of the injured out on verandas when wards were filled to capacity.

The white authorities' attitude to the massacre was probably summed up by the statement of local police commander, Col. D.H. Pienaar, who said: 'It started when hordes of natives *(sic)* surrounded the police station. If they do these things, they must learn their lesson the hard way.'

In a similar disturbance, in the township of Langa near Cape Town, a further seven protesters died and more than 200 were injured. Four days later, on March 25, all black political groups were banned by the government in Johannesburg and, two days later, African National Congress leader Chief Luthuli began a new campaign of destroying passbooks by symbolically burning his own.

On March 30, a state of emergency was declared as tens of thousands of black dissidents demanded the release of all protest leaders held in custody. It was clear that British Prime Minister Harold Macmillan's 'wind of change' speech in February had been sadly prophetic. Sharpeville was the turning point.

London To Have Flood Barrier

Constantly threatened by the possibility of flooding at times when high tides coincide with storm conditions, London was offered a lifeline today with the announcement that a government study recommended that a movable barrier be built across the River Thames. Although it was seven years since Central London was last hit by the mix of conditions which could have overrun worn-out sea defences, the threat was obviously considered real enough to warrant a government order to engineers to find a solution. The two main options were a swing-bridge or a lifting gate construction. Either way, it was estimated that the project would cost about £17 million ($42m) to complete, and would take around six years.

MARCH 16

King Wins Concessions From Ike

Confirmation of the Rev. Dr Martin Luther King's position as undisputed leader and chief spokesman for the US civil rights movement came in Washington today when President Eisenhower conceded to his demands that he should lend his weight to preventing an escalation of racial tension in Alabama, where more than a thousand black students had staged a peaceful demo against segregation in Montgomery, on March 1.

The President's suggestion - that committees composed of black and white members should be set up in the States where tension was especially high, and black complaints should be allowed to be publicly aired - wasn't much. But it was presidential recognition of Dr King's influence.

MARCH 29

US And UK Agree Nuclear Test Treaty

With an East-West summit conference scheduled to take place in May, US President Eisenhower and British Prime Minister Macmillan today agreed an Anglo-US nuclear test-ban treaty to present to Russia in the form of proposals.

The deal, which was finalized at the President's Camp David retreat, will see the Western powers offering a short-term moratorium on underground tests, in return for a formal, long-term treaty banning all other nuclear explosions.

THREE-OSCAR WILDER SCORES WITH 'THE APARTMENT'

This year's Academy Awards ceremony gave the Austrian-born Billy Wilder the unprecedented pleasure of stepping up on three occasions to collect well-deserved Oscars as producer, director and writer of *The Apartment*. Like a number of his creations *(Double Indemnity, Sunset Boulevard* and *Some Like It Hot* included), *The Apartment* would quickly graduate to 'classic' status and continue to provide future generations of writers, directors and actors with a superb masterclass in all those skills.

Which makes it odd that *The Apartment* star Jack Lemmon missed out on the Best Actor award, which went to Burt Lancaster for his powerful portrayal of the maverick preacher Elmer Gantry, while his co-star Shirley Maclaine lost out in the Best Actress stakes to Elizabeth Taylor's high-class call-girl with the phone number prefix *Butterfield 8*.

As ever, Miss Taylor managed to dominate press coverage of the evening. Having, in a short 12 months, transformed herself from producer Mike Todd's grieving widow to the homebreaking tramp who'd stolen singer Eddie Fisher (her *Butterfield 8* co-star) from actress Debbie Reynolds, and spent a month in a London clinic after an emergency tracheotomy, La Taylor collected her Oscar for a role she'd condemned as 'salacious trash' before reluctantly accepting it, in a movie she was still describing as 'a real stinker'!

While the epic history re-write *The Alamo* was nominated in the Best Picture category, director-star John Wayne didn't get a mention in the sections where he ought, by any process of logic, to have been a contender.

The reverse was true of the chiller-thriller and box office smash *Psycho*. If director Alfred Hitchcock merited a nomination as Best Director, how come the film itself wasn't short-listed as Best Film? And, while Janet Leigh (whose part in the film ended fairly early when she was murdered in her motel shower) was nominated as Best Supporting Actress, leading man Anthony Perkins (who carried the film with his twitchy Norman Bates) didn't make the Best Actor list.

The year's other blockbuster, *Spartacus,* packed cinemas the world over, but failed to win any nominations for its director or for its stars. Peter Ustinov did collect the Best Supporting Actor award for his oily slave-dealer, and cinematographer Russell Metty, art directors Alexander Golitzen and Eric Osborn, and costume designers Valles and Bill Thomas did pick up Oscars.

Gary Cooper's impending death was predicted by his award of an Honorary Oscar. Stan Laurel's death was marked with a posthumous ditto, while Walt Disney's lobbyists had worked overtime to gain Britain's teen star Hayley Mills another Honorary Oscar for 'outstanding juvenile performance'.

The song of the year? It went to *Never On A Sunday,* of course!

Laurence Olivier, Tony Curtis and Peter Ustinov
during the filming of 'Spartacus'

East Germans Flood Into West Berlin

MORE THAN 5,000 EAST GERMANS were reported to have crossed into West Berlin in the past few days - many of them smallholding farmers said to be unhappy with the Communist regime's imposition of collective farming - to create the greatest mass exodus since the East Berlin rising of 1953.

Resources in West Berlin reception centres, which were used to coping with no more than 300 people a day, were overwhelmed by the 'invasion', and two former refugee camps had to be reopened. The authorities also had to suspend the usual screening procedure which aimed to identify and isolate communist 'plants', sending as many people into West Germany as they could.

One of the biggest headaches facing West Germany would be how to cope with the arrival of so many landless farmers and agricultural workers. It was going to prove difficult, if not impossible, to absorb them into a population already burdened with thousands of earlier refugees still waiting for work and land.

1: My Old Man's A Dustman
- Lonnie Donegan
2: Fall In Love With You
- Cliff Richard
3: Handy Man
- Jimmy Jones
4: Do You Mind
- Anthony Newley
5: Fings Ain't What They Used To Be
- Max Bygraves
6: Stuck On You
- Elvis Presley
7: Theme From 'A Summer Place'
- Percy Faith
8: Running Bear
- Johnny Preston
9: Beatnik Fly
- Johnny & The Hurricanes
10: Someone Else's Baby
- Adam Faith

APRIL 10

Rivals Form 'Stop JFK' Group

Following his recent victory in the Democratic Party's primary in Wisconsin, a new coalition was announced in Washington today, with the aim of defeating Senator John F. Kennedy in next month's West Virginia primary and ensuring a presidential candidacy nomination for Hubert Humphrey.

Fronted by arch-conservative Senator Robert Byrd, the group's main line of attack was to be Kennedy's youth and inexperience, though the subject of his Roman Catholic faith would be a strong subtext. Kennedy would confront the issue head-on, making it clear that he believed that State and Church should be completely separated.

APRIL 5

Heston's Epic Reaps Record Oscar Harvest

Tonight's Academy Awards ceremony in Hollywood turned into a record-breaking victory procession for *Ben Hur,* the $4 million epic starring Charlton Heston, Jack Hawkins, Stephen Boyd, Hugh Griffith, Finlay Currie and a supporting cast of up to a thousand others.

The film won an astonishing ten Oscars to emerge the runaway hit of the party held to honour the 1959 crop of the world's cinematic creations.

Perhaps one or more of the trio of stars - Rock Hudson, Marlon Brando and Burt Lancaster - who'd turned down the title role regretted their decision when the film took the Oscars by storm, and Heston stepped up to accept his Best Actor statuette.

APRIL 2

'Tiros' Improves World Weather Picture

The world's first weather satellite, *Tiros 1,* took the first step towards making forecasting a less imprecise science today when it began sending pictures back to earth from its orbit 450 miles in space. The first pictures were of the cloud cover over the north-eastern United States and part of Canada.

Launched by NASA last month, *Tiros* was destined to be the prototype for a series of weather labs which would give all-round coverage of the global meteorological situation and help scientists predict the build-up of severe phenomena like hurricanes and typhoons.

APRIL 9

Verwoerd Shot As South African Turmoil Continues

DR HENDRIK VERWOERD, the South African Prime Minister and symbol of apartheid, was shot and seriously injured today, only moments after he had sat down after speaking at the Johannesburg Agricultural Show. His would-be assassin was a wealthy white farmer, David Pratt, who had recently been refused a visa to leave South Africa and visit his estranged wife in Holland.

Verwoerd's shooting came as South Africa reeled from a series of anti-apartheid riots in the wake of the Sharpeville massacre and the mass round-up of black politicians which had followed.

On April 7, police fired into a crowd of 1,000 blacks said to be attacking people in Durban as they tried to defy a general-strike call made by the Pan-African Congress. Another incident saw a crowd armed with iron bars, sticks and axes force its way into a Durban shopping centre, with police gunfire used to scatter a group said to be headed for the city's jail, temporary 'home' for a number of African leaders. Three protesters were reported killed.

The African township of Nyanga, near Cape Town, was cordoned off after a black police officer was hacked to death. A baby was killed when a soldier fired into a car trying to reverse away from a roadblock. The child's parents had been attempting to reach a nearby hospital and were obeying an order to go back when the shot was fired.

Unlike the child, Hendrik Verwoerd would recover from his injuries.

APRIL 18

Rock Star Cochran Killed In Taxi Crash

The pop world was stunned today as it learned that American rock 'n' roll star Eddie Cochran - seriously injured yesterday when a taxi carrying him, his fiancée Sharon Sheeley and fellow rock star Gene Vincent crashed at high speed in the Wiltshire town of Chippenham - had died from his injuries.

Only 22 years old, Cochran had been touring Britain with Vincent, a tour which had confirmed his position as one of the most popular and accomplished rock performers. The biggest hits of his relatively short career included *Summertime Blues*, *C'Mon Everybody* and *20 Flight Rock*, all of which he wrote.

Cochran, Miss Sheeley and Vincent were *en route* to Heathrow Airport and a return to the US when the taxi they'd hired to take them from Bristol to London went out of control and crashed into a concrete lamppost. The driver and another passenger escaped unscathed, but the three Americans were all hurt - Sheeley suffering back injuries, and Vincent a fractured collar-bone - with Cochran receiving severe lacerations to his brain.

The young performer's body was flown to Los Angeles a few days later and he was buried on April 25. With the macabre irony which seems to attach itself to the sudden death of pop artists, Cochran's newly-released single was entitled *Three Steps To Heaven*.

APRIL 27

Riots Force Out Korea's Rhee

Once the undisputed strong-man of South Korea, the 85-year-old President, Synghman Rhee, finally resigned today after a week of disturbances in the capital, Seoul, left 115 student protesters dead. The riots had been sparked by Rhee's victory in last month's elections, which many believed had been fixed to ensure he enjoyed a fourth successive term in office. His position became impossible when the US attacked the 'repressive measures' he adopted to quell demonstrations reflecting 'popular dissatisfaction'.

APRIL 13

'Who Do You Think You Are - Stirling Moss?'

It was a phrase about to enter the British vocabulary as the standard question asked by traffic police of anyone breaking the speed limit, and it came about as a result of a court hearing today.

In the dock and found guilty of dangerous driving, British Grand Prix star Stirling Moss had his driving-licence suspended for a year, banning him from driving on public roads in that time. It did not affect his ability or eligibility to continue tearing around the world's circuits at whatever speeds he wanted, however.

21

Soviets Shoot Down U-2 Plane - US Denies Spying

THE EVER-COOL ATMOSPHERE between the world's two superpowers turned decidedly frosty today when an American U-2 aircraft was shot out of the sky while in Russian airspace. Soviet leader Nikita Khrushchev justified the action by claiming that the aircraft's course had been a deliberate violation intended to disrupt the summit conference between the United States, the Soviet Union, Great Britain and France, due to take place less than two weeks later.

It quickly became clear that the Russians suspected that the U-2 was on a spying mission, a charge the US State Department just as quickly denied. The flight had merely been for collecting meteorological data, it said, and the 30-year-old pilot, Gary Powers, was a civilian who'd simply strayed off course.

The presence of a camera on the plane? For photographing clouds, said Washington. For filming military installations, said Moscow. While both claims appeared plausible, the episode dashed hopes anyone may have had of an early end to the cold war.

The Paris summit - which was attended by US President Dwight Eisenhower, Mr Khrushchev, French President Charles de Gaulle and British Prime Minister Harold Macmillan - was to last a mere three days before it broke up on May 17 without going into full session.

A righteously indignant Khrushchev demanded a public apology from Eisenhower - and an assurance that there would be no further intrusions on Russian airspace - before he would sit down with the others. When his demands were met with an equally indignant denial from Eisenhower, the summit broke up.

Queen Mother Hails 'Symbolic' Kariba Dam

Queen Elizabeth, the Queen Mother, pressed a switch today to start the hydro-electric turbines of the Kariba Dam, the massive structure built by the Central African Federation of Rhodesia and Nyasaland to harness the natural power of the Zambezi River.

Describing the dam as 'a marvel of modern engineering which in future may rank with the Seven Wonders of the Ancient World', the Queen Mother said she prayed that Kariba would also become 'the symbol of a new and wider understanding throughout the federation'.

MAY 6

London Greets Margaret, The Princess Bride

Thousands of Londoners today confirmed that royal occasions - especially weddings - remained a prime attraction and a good excuse for enthusiastic celebration, when they packed the streets of the capital to catch a glimpse of Princess Margaret riding in a coach from Buckingham Palace to her wedding at Westminster Abbey.

It was the first royal marriage since her older sister, then Princess Elizabeth, married Lieutenant Philip Mountbatten, the newly-titled Duke of Edinburgh, in 1947. Princess Margaret's bridegroom, photographer Antony Armstrong-Jones, would cease to be a commoner when the Queen awarded him the title Lord Snowdon.

MAY 16

MPs Vote To Curb Teddy Boys

In the House of Commons today, Members of Parliament gave a second unopposed reading to a government bill to curb Teddy boys, the gangs of Edwardian-styled dandies who first achieved notoriety for fights inspired by British screenings of the movie *Rock Around The Clock* in 1956.

It is difficult, in retrospect, to credit that the government apparently agreed to introduce a bill to control Teddy boys. Elvis had been in the army. Buddy Holly and Eddie Cochran were dead. Bill Haley was history and Jerry Lee Lewis was in disgrace for marrying his cousin, who was only 13 years old.

Teddy boys - and the original rebellious rock 'n' roll - were such a spent force, they didn't need curbing.

UK TOP 10 SINGLES

1: Cathy's Clown
- The Everly Brothers
2: Someone Else's Baby
- Adam Faith
3: Handy Man
- Jimmy Jones
4: Do You Mind
- Anthony Newley
5: Sweet Nothin's
- Brenda Lee
6: Cradle Of Love
- Johnny Preston
7: Shazam!
- Duane Eddy
8: Fall In Love With You
- Cliff Richard
9: Standing On The Corner
- The King Brothers
10: Footsteps
- Steve Lawrence

MAY 23

Israelis Capture Death Camp Boss Eichmann

ADOLF EICHMANN, the SS officer generally recognized as the man who supervised Hitler's 'Final Solution' to exterminate more than six million Jews and other 'undesirables', was today reported to be in Israel - captured by Israeli intelligence agents and about to face charges which carried the death penalty.

Announcing the news to a startled and suddenly silent Knesset, Israeli Prime Minister David Ben-Gurion described Eichmann as 'one of the greatest of the Nazi war criminals', which was certainly not meant as a compliment.

No details were provided of how Eichmann's arrest was made, but local sources suggested that the Israeli secret service kidnapped him in Argentina, where he and other prominent Nazis were known to be living under assumed names. The government in Buenos Aires would demand his return two weeks later, but the Israelis would not release a man who had managed to evade capture on a number of previous occasions.

Real Madrid Win Fifth European Cup

Spanish champions Real Madrid made an indelible mark on the history of football this month in Glasgow when, in a Hampden Park Stadium packed with 128,000 fans, they thrashed West German champions Eintracht 7-3 to win the European Cup for the fifth time in succession.

Real's remarkable achievement, never to be challenged since, came via four goals from Hungarian veteran Ferenc Puskas and a hat trick from their captain, the Argentinian superstar Alfredo Di Stefano. The latter made the record books in his own right, having scored in all of Real's previous finals against Stade de Reims (in 1956 and 1959), Fiorentina (in 1957) and Milan (in 1958).

MAY 17

Humphrey Throws In The Towel

Soundly beaten by John F. Kennedy in the Democratic Party's Wisconsin, Nebraska and West Virginia primaries, Senator Hubert Humphrey's bid to become a presidential election candidate ended officially today when Kennedy won 70 per cent of the votes cast in the Maryland primary. Announcing his retirement from the race, and promising his full support for the Kennedy campaign, the senator effectively confirmed that the November presidential election would be a two-horse race between the Republicans' obvious choice, Vice-President Richard Nixon, and the young senator from Massachusetts.

MAY 31

'Dr Zhivago' Author Pasternak Dies

Boris Pasternak, the acclaimed author best known for the epic Russian Revolution novel, *Dr Zhivago,* died today in his villa outside Moscow. He was 70 years old.

Although his novel was banned in his own country, it helped win him the supreme accolade of the Nobel Prize for Literature, an award the Soviet Government 'persuaded' him to decline. Pasternak also announced that he would never accept royalties from the book's publication outside the USSR.

Pasternak was, in fact, better known in Russia for his lyric poetry, work which dried up during Stalin's regime when he published only poetic translations of Shakespeare's plays.

JUNE

JUNE 12

Sikhs Arrested In Homeland Demos

One of the biggest demonstrations by Sikhs demanding their own homeland, with a legislature entirely separate from the rest of India, saw the centre of the Indian capital, New Delhi, paralysed for hours and more than 780 protesters arrested.

With their own religion, language and traditions, the Sikh homeland movement had grown in intensity over the past few years, with the most fanatical members prepared to suffer martyrdom for their cause. So, a few hours fighting with baton-wielding police was nothing much to boast about, and a spell in prison was a small price to pay.

Two Killed At Indy 500

Notorious as one of the world's most dangerous motor-races, the Indianapolis 500 usually takes its toll on the drivers and cars that take part in the American classic. This month's event was different.
Two spectators died and dozens were injured when an aluminium tower collapsed as the annual spectacle unfolded. Officials said it was sheer chance that more were not killed in the accident - the tower missed a large stand, with hundreds more race fans, only by a matter of feet.

JUNE 2

London Calls For High-Rise Rethink

London's city planners today announced a set of eight new rules intended to control the number of high-rise buildings - offices and blocks of flats - which had transformed the capital's skyline.

Occupying hundreds of sites left derelict by wartime bombs, the new flats had come in for special criticism. Although there was a desperate need for new low-rent accommodation in the docklands area of East London, many people who'd been relocated missed their old close-knit communities and felt marooned in the new tower blocks.

The London County Council planners wanted new projects to meet aesthetic standards which would make them blend better with existing buildings and include open spaces.

Lumumba Outburst Sours Congo Independence Party

THE COSY CUSTOM of celebrating independence with anodyne speeches was unceremoniously ignored in the former Belgian Congo today when the country's first Prime Minister, Patrice Lumumba, told King Baudouin and stunned VIPs precisely what the people of the Congo had been forced to endure during 80 years of Belgian rule.

In his speech, which followed King Baudouin's homily stressing how much his country had provided for the Congo in that time, and his presentation to Lumumba of the Belgian Order of Leopold, the new PM launched into a catalogue of complaints against the Congo's former overlords.

'We had to submit to ironies, insults and blows day and night because we were black,' he railed, as the king looked stonily ahead. 'In towns there were magnificent houses for whites, while there were only broken-down hovels for blacks.'

'A black man was not allowed into cinemas, restaurants and shops,' he continued. 'The black man paraded on foot like a hen, while the whites travelled in luxury in motor cars.' President Joseph Kasavubu, who appointed Lumumba, was believed to be regretting his choice as he persuaded King Baudouin and Belgian cabinet ministers to attend the official lunch which followed.

UK TOP 10 SINGLES

1: Cathy's Clown
- The Everly Brothers
2: Cradle Of Love
- Johnny Preston
3: Handy Man
- Jimmy Jones
4: Three Steps To Heaven
- Eddie Cochran
5: Sweet Nothin's
- Brenda Lee
6: Robot Man
- Connie Francis
7: I Wanna Go Home
- Lonnie Donegan
8: Shazam!
- Duane Eddy
9: Mama
- Connie Francis
10: Someone Else's Baby
- Adam Faith

Communist World Split As Khrushchev And Mao Trade Insults

JUNE 22

RECENT HINTS OF A MAJOR SPLIT between the world's two biggest Communist countries, the Soviet Union and China, overflowed into a public slanging-match this month when their leaders accused each other of philosophical and political mistakes.

First to go into action was Russian leader Nikita Khrushchev. Addressing the Romanian Communist Party conference in Bucharest on June 22, Khrushchev was almost as scathing about Chinese Chairman Mao Tse-tung as he had been a few weeks earlier about US President Eisenhower, accusing Mao of being 'another Stalin' and claiming that China did not understand the terrible implications of a modern war.

Chairman Mao responded in kind, dubbing Khrushchev a revisionist who failed to appreciate the real strength of imperialism. The two had been sparring for months via carefully scripted press articles, but Khrushchev's outburst was the first known public statement of his hatred of Mao.

Such sabre-rattling, said some commentators, did not augur well for world peace. Not so, said others. If Russia and China ever became allies, communism would control most of the Northern hemisphere, an even less appealing prospect than the present uneasy truce between Russia and America, with China forced to concentrate its energies on solving its own internal problems of overpopulation and industrial under-achievement.

JUNE 20

Patterson Pounds Swede To Regain World Title

American fighter Floyd Patterson tonight became the first man ever to regain boxing's ultimate prize - the world heavyweight title - when he floored Swedish champion Ingemar Johansson with a left hook in the fifth round.

Patterson had lost his crown to Johansson in June 1959, when the largely unknown and unfancied Johansson knocked him to the canvas seven times before the fight was stopped by the referee. Patterson's victory returned the insult with interest as he knocked out the only non-American holder of the title since the 1930s.

Watch Out! There's A Psycho About!

Doing absolutely nothing for the commission earnings of bathroom shower salesmen, but about to do a world of good for Britain's cinemas trying to stem the flood of audiences switching to television, Alfred Hitchcock's new chiller thriller, *Psycho*, made its London début tonight, winning universal praise for its heart-stopping story - especially that shower scene.

The psychopath dreamed up by British-born Hitchcock was Norman Bates, a motel-owner (played by Anthony Perkins) who took an unnatural fancy to a runaway Janet Leigh. What would his mother say?

All Change For British Motor Industry

One famous British motor car marque disappeared this month and another changed hands during ten days which saw the shape of the luxury end of the UK car industry change dramatically.

The Armstrong Siddeley company, one of the oldest British quality motor manufacturers, announced it was to cease production on June 10, driven out of business by competition from its bigger and more successful rivals. And on June 19, the similarly venerable Daimler (of German parentage, but active in Britain since the end of the nineteenth century) merged with the fashionably fast Jaguar company. It was understood that Jaguar paid around £3.5 million ($7m) to acquire Daimler, with plans to continue building Daimler cars and buses - as well as the celebrated Daimler hearse, without which no respectable funeral was considered complete.

WORLD'S ATHLETES BEAT ROME'S HEAT TO CREATE MEMORABLE OLYMPICS

It's hard to understand how anyone involved in the staging of the 1960 Olympic Games in Rome could have thought that August - the height of the Mediterranean summer - was an appropriate time to ask the world's leading athletes to deliver their best. But they did, and many of those who took part were able to overcome conditions which claimed the life of a Danish cyclist found to have taken a banned stimulant before his road-race.

The first Games to be televised worldwide, the performances of Southern hemisphere middle-distance runners did much to boost viewing figures in New Zealand and Australia. Kiwi Peter Snell beat the Belgian world record holder, Roger Moens, to take the 800m gold medal, Australian ace Herb Elliott established a new world record of 3 mins 35.6 secs while winning the 1500m, and New Zealand's Murray Halberg saw off the challenge of West Germany's Hans Grodotzki to take the 5000m gold.

If the US men surprisingly failed to win the sprints - David Sime losing out to West Germany's Armin Hary in the 100m, and Lebster Carney being outpaced by local hero Livio Berruti in the 200m - Otis Davis did at least salvage some American pride by taking the 400m gold.

The acknowledged athletics star of the 1960 Games turned out to be the Tennessee-born beauty Wilma Rudolph, who struck gold not only in the 100m and 200m, but also as a member of the victorious US 4x100m relay team. Her achievements were particularly remarkable as Rudolph had suffered from polio as a child, and had been unable to walk until her ninth year.

Also remarkable was the victory of Ethiopian Abebe Bikila in the marathon - running barefoot to win Africa's first-ever track and field gold medal. Unsurprisingly, given the average temperatures in his homeland, Bikila was reported as saying that he still felt fresh enough to complete the course a second time, although he'd already broken the world record during his win.

The heat was generally blamed for the almost complete failure of the British athletics team, whose only major success was London office-worker Don Thompson's gold medal in the 50km walk. The astonishingly dedicated 'Mighty Mouse' (as the British press immediately dubbed the bespectacled, fragile-looking athlete) was apparently smart enough to improvise the climate he would find in Rome by training in his steam-filled bathroom!

With the benefit of hindsight, the crowning of the young American boxer Cassius Clay as Olympic light heavyweight boxing champion was a taste of the many delights the world could expect from a precocious and gifted fighter. Watching his victory over Poland's Zbigniew Pietrykowski was a consortium of Kentucky businessmen prepared to underwrite Clay's professional career - and we all know how that turned out…

Cassius Clay

THE SPORTS YEAR IN BRIEF

AMERICAN FOOTBALL

In a dramatic year of change, the LA Rams' general manager Pete Rozelle was appointed Commissioner of the NFL, which granted a franchise to the newly-formed Dallas Cowboys.

A rival organization, the AFL, was officially formed, with the Dallas Texans' Lamar Hunt appointed President. He scored an immediate winning touchdown by negotiating a five-year TV deal with ABC worth $9 million.

GOLF

Australian Kel Nagle stopped Arnold Palmer scoring a remarkable treble (he'd already won the US Masters and the US Open this year) at the British Open, at Royal Lytham. Arnie's US Open win saw him haul back a last-round deficit of seven strokes to overnight leader Mike Souchak, and five to Ben Hogan, with a round of 65 which included six birdies at the first seven holes. He ended 1960 as the leading money-winner with $75,262.

MOTOR-RACING

Another Australian victory as Jack Brabham won his second successive World Championship with the British Cooper-Climax team. Their dominance was typified by the 1-2-3-4 clean sweep in the French Grand Prix.

Tragedy struck the Belgian GP at Spa when Stirling Moss was badly injured in a practice crash, the British driver Mike Taylor died in practice, and the race itself was marred by the deaths of two other Brits, Lotus works driver Alan Stacy and Stirling Moss's protégé Chris Cooper, a Cooper team member.

Chichester Beats Cancer And Storms To Set Atlantic Record

NEW YORK RIVERSIDE WORKERS crammed the banks of the Hudson today to welcome one of the bravest men ever to sail into their waters. The object of their applause – lone British sailor Francis Chichester, who had just set a new transatlantic record of 40 days from Plymouth to the New World.

Their congratulations were well-deserved. The 58-year-old hero had learned he was suffering from lung cancer two years earlier, and his epic voyage was the best way he knew to prove he wasn't beaten.

The Atlantic did its best to prove him wrong, however. Chichester's 39-foot sloop, *Gypsy Moth II,* had to battle against hurricane-force winds for part of the voyage, and his clothes were so battered, torn and soaked, he'd been forced to abandon his plan to wear a dinner-jacket when he took his evening meal!

Britain Loses Nye, Rebel Architect Of National Health

Aneurin Bevan, the fiery socialist who helped mastermind the creation of Britain's National Health Service in 1945, and who revelled in his role as the Labour Party's chief rebel, died today, aged 62. With his death, Britain lost one of its most gifted and controversial politicians and a brilliant orator fired by the depth of his convictions.

(See Came & Went pages)

World's First Woman PM Sworn In

The world's first democratically elected woman Prime Minister, Mrs Sirimavo Bandaranaike, was sworn into office today in Ceylon.

The widow of Solomon Bandaranaike - Ceylon's Prime Minister from 1956 until he was assassinated in September last year - she made history when her Sri Lanka Freedom Party won 75 of the 150 seats in the recent general election.

Mrs Bandaranaike only entered politics after her husband's death, promising to continue with the reforms he had begun, and describing these as 'socialist programmes which reflect the national aspirations of the people'.

Congo Torn By Civil War As Katanga Splits

Only 11 days old, the newly-independent Congo Republic faced disintegration and chaos today when the copper-rich province of Katanga declared its own independence under Moise Tshombe, a businessman who'd moved into politics after three bankruptcies.

Belgian paratroops, flown into Katanga three days earlier at the request of the Congo's President, Joseph Kasavubu, faced a hail of bullets, stones and other missiles as they tried to quell rioting in Elizabethville, the provincial capital, where ten Europeans were reported killed.

As Belgian nationals fled in their thousands over the River Congo to Brazzaville, they accused the Brussels government of abandoning them. On July 15, UN troops would begin arriving in the Congo in a move inspired by UN Secretary-General Dag Hammarskjöld.

1: Good Timin'
- Jimmy Jones
2: Please Don't Tease
- Cliff Richard
3: Ain't Misbehavin'
- Tommy Bruce & The Bruisers
4: Shakin' All Over
- Johnny Kidd & The Pirates
5: What A Mouth
- Tommy Steele
6: Robot Man
- Connie Francis
7: Made You
- Adam Faith
8: Three Steps To Heaven
- Eddie Cochran
9: Angela Jones
- Michael Cox
10: Look For A Star
- Garry Mills

ARRIVALS

Born this month:
1: Evelyn 'Champagne' King, US pop singer
11: Richie Sambora, US rock guitarist (Bon Jovi)
20: Jonathan Morris, UK stage and TV actor (*Bread, Me & My Girl,* etc.)
26: Danny Stagg, UK rock musician (Kingdom Come)
27: Jo(sephine) Durie, UK tennis player

DEPARTURES

Died this month:
6: Aneurin Bevan, UK socialist politician *(see main story)*

JULY 27

Supermac Promotes Home And Heath

British Prime Minister Harold Macmillan today increased the immediate status and long-term career prospects of two men he considered both able and loyal, when he carried out a mid-term cabinet reshuffle.

Promoted to the key post of Foreign Secretary was Alec Douglas-Home, the Earl of Home, who'd served as Minister of Commonwealth Relations since 1955.

His deputy was to be Edward Heath, MP for Bexley since 1950 but, more importantly, the Conservative Party's Chief Whip since 1955. His skill in maintaining party discipline after the 1956 Suez fiasco had not gone unnoticed, nor unrewarded.

Aussies Capture Sporting Headlines

A two-day display of strength in depth saw Australian sportsmen capture back-page headlines this month.
On July 2, Neale Fraser and Rod Laver battled it out in the Wimbledon Men's Final to see whose name would be added to the historic trophy. In fact, Fraser - beaten finalist in 1958 - overcame the skills of Laver - defeated last year by Olmedo - to emerge the 6-4,3-6,9-7,7-5 champion.
On July 3, current Formula One man-to-beat Jack Brabham added the French Grand Prix trophy to his growing stock of silverware, giving the folks Down Under another reason to crack a tinny or two.

Kennedy Evokes Golden Age To Launch New Frontier

VICTORIOUS IN HIS BID to become the Democratic Party's presidential candidate in the forthcoming election, John F. Kennedy improved his stock with the floating voters of America with a stirring acceptance speech which called for the nation to move to what he called 'a new frontier'.

Speaking at the Democrats' Los Angeles Convention, Kennedy linked himself in spirit with the two outstanding Democratic Presidents of this century - Woodrow Wilson, who was in the White House during the First World War, and Franklin D. Roosevelt, who contributed greatly to Allied success in the Second World War, and died in 1945, just before that success became outright victory.

Kennedy recalled Roosevelt's famous 'New Deal' initiative of 1933 which gave ordinary Americans renewed hope in the aftermath of the 1929 Wall Street Crash, when 13 million shares changed hands in one day.

His 'new frontier' was not a set of promises, Kennedy stressed, but rather a set of challenges which he believed would appeal to the frontier spirit which had enabled previous generations to settle the remote lands of the West and build a new country.

In an astute move calculated to broaden his electoral base in the South, Kennedy chose Senator Lyndon Johnson, the Texan he'd beaten to win the Democratic nomination, as his vice-presidential running mate. On July 27, their expected opponent was confirmed when the Republican Party Convention in Chicago nominated Vice-President Richard Nixon to be its champion in the coming fight.

Bing Gets Platinum Award

A momentous day for veteran crooner Bing Crosby when his mountainous record sales were officially recognized by a grateful music industry.

Bing's astonishing 200 million total was marked with the presentation to him of a solid platinum disc - the first in music business history.

AUGUST 19

Soviets Find U-2 Pilot Powers Guilty Of Spying

AMERICAN PILOT GARY POWERS,
(pictured) whose U-2 aircraft was shot down
near a Soviet arms centre in May, was today
found guilty of espionage and sentenced to ten
years' detention - at least seven of them to be
served in a labour camp.

Powers, who had pleaded guilty, claiming he
was acting on orders from the US Central
Intelligence Agency, showed no reaction as an
interpreter explained the judgement to him.

The high-flying U-2 reconnaissance plane was
hit by a ground-to-air missile after it was tracked
over Soviet missile sites and arms factories.
Powers had taken off on his fateful mission from
a US air-base in Pakistan, never dreaming that it
would lead to the collapse of the Paris summit
between the so-called Big Four powers - the
United States, Soviet Russia, Britain and France -
and a scheduled visit to the USSR by President
Eisenhower.

Powers would languish in Russia until February
1962, when he would be exchanged for captured
KGB Colonel Rudolph Abel in the first
acknowledged East-West spy swap.

Penguin's 'Lady C' Plans Thwarted By Summons

The plans of leading paperback publishers Penguin Books to produce the first ever uncensored, or 'unexpurgated', British edition of *Lady Chatterley's Lover,* the sexually explicit novel by D.H. Lawrence, were frozen today when the company learned that the Director of Public Prosecutions (DPP) was considering legal action against it and them.

Written 30 years earlier, but available only in a much-cut version ever since, *Lady Chatterley's Lover* had been viewed as now acceptable after Penguin's lawyers had a close look at the small print of the 1959 Obscene Publications Act, the first piece of written legislation attempting to define what was art, and what was just dirty.

The rumour-mill proved correct. On August 19, officials of the DPP served Penguin with a summons. A High Court hearing was set to begin in October, when everyone expected sparks to fly. They would not be disappointed.

Laos Coup Puts Prince Back In Power

Prince Souvanna Phouma returned to the post of Prime Minister of Laos today, his position secured in a coup by a paratroop force led by Captain Kong Le.

The Prince was PM for a short period three years ago, when he created a coalition with the pro-communist Laos Patriotic Front before being ousted.

During the intervening period, Laos, which borders Vietnam to the east, had been largely pro-Western, but observers believed that the new government would seek the safety and calm of neutrality.

UK TOP 10 SINGLES

1: Please Don't Tease
- Cliff Richard
2: Apache
- The Shadows
3: A Mess Of Blues
- Elvis Presley
4: Shakin' All Over
- Johnny Kidd & The Pirates
5: Because They're Young
- Duane Eddy
6: When Will I Be Loved
- The Everly Brothers
7: Good Timin'
- Jimmy Jones
8: If She Should Come To You
- Anthony Newley
9: Tie Me Kangaroo Down, Sport
- Rolf Harris
10: Itsy Bitsy Teenie Weenie Yellow Polka Dot Bikini
- Brian Hyland

Student Satire Is Edinburgh Festival Hit

The Edinburgh Festival fringe, long noted for its innovation, had that reputation reinforced this month by a revue titled *Beyond The Fringe* which gained critical acclaim for its freshness, wit and refusal to be impressed by tradition.

Featuring four Oxbridge students - Alan Bennett, Peter Cook, Jonathan Miller and Dudley Moore - *Beyond The Fringe* sketches revealed an anti-establishment bias which often overflowed into ridicule, a tongue-in-cheek approach which made it especially popular with younger members of its audience.

At the end of its Edinburgh season, it was announced that *Beyond The Fringe* would have the rare distinction of being transferred to a major London theatre.

The Wobble-Board? Rolf Explains All!

As his wacky *Tie Me Kangaroo Down, Sport* became Britain's novelty hit of the year, Australian singer and comedian Rolf Harris was pressed from all sides to explain precisely how he played the wobble-board - the unique percussion 'instrument' he invented and played on the single.

Readers of British pop paper *The New Musical Express* were the first to benefit from a step-by-step guide Harris prepared for them. It went like this:

Step 1: Locate a piece of hardboard three feet long and 18 inches wide.

Step 2: Grasp both ends of the board firmly in your hand.

Step 3: With a flick of the wrists, bend the board up and down to produce a rhythmic 'whoolp' and 'beloop'.

Step 4: Become rich and famous.

AUGUST 25

Rome Olympics Open

In the sweltering heat of an Italian summer, the Olympic Games officially opened in Rome today. Its timing and the unyielding conditions which inevitably confronted outdoor competitors in daytime events were heavily criticized by commentators and athletes alike. As usual, however, the Games produced their fair share of superlatives, surprises and stars of the future.

(See Sports pages for full details)

AUGUST 16

Wary Cypriots Shun Independence Ceremony

THE PEOPLE OF CYPRUS, the Mediterranean island nation which finally achieved independence at midnight tonight with a traditional 21-gun salute, speeches and the raising of a new national flag, did not observe the historic moment with the enthusiasm expected on such occasions.

With the island still rent by the activities of Greek and Turkish terrorists, there was assumed to be a risk of violence as one side or the other decided to mark the transition with riots or bombs.

In the event, the official ceremony went off uninterrupted as the departing British Governor, Sir Hugh Foot, appealed for peace. 'People who have been at the edge of hell do not want to go back,' he said, before handing power of government to the new President, Greek community leader Archbishop Makarios, and his deputy, the Turkish-Cypriot Dr Kutchuk.

AUGUST 20

Belgian Troops Quit Congo As UN Moves In

The Congo crisis deepened and became more confused this month as the actions of the rebel Katanga province dictated events and threw the country into a full-scale civil war.

On August 3, Katangan leader Moise Tshombe decided the UN troops who'd replaced Belgian forces last month were every bit the enemy the old colonial forces had been, and ordered his military commanders to begin a series of guerrilla raids.

Convinced that the United Nations could effect a solution by being even-handed, Secretary-General Dag Hammarskjöld acted decisively on August 8, ordering Belgian troops out of the Congo altogether. Only too happy to get out of an increasingly impossible situation, the Brussels government agreed and, on August 14, Swedish UN troops replaced the Belgians.

Determined to stamp his authority on a rapidly deteriorating scenario, on August 16 Congolese Prime Minister Patrice Lumumba declared a state of martial law for the next six months.

HANK AND CO. START DRIFTING OUT OF CLIFF'S SHADOW

The only mystery surrounding the emergence of The Shadows as Britain's most successful group before The Beatles was: why did it take them until July this year to enjoy their first hit single? As featured backing group for the country's biggest singing star, with a segment of their own in his sell-out concerts, the three singles they'd released prior to *Apache* should have enjoyed a better showing in the charts.

Then they were called The Drifters, which they changed to avoid confusion with the American group of the same name. There had also been a line-up change or two, but it was the quartet comprising lead guitarist Hank B. Marvin, rhythm guitarist Bruce Welch, bassist Jet Harris and drummer Tony Meehan who recorded *Apache* as The Shadows to begin a remarkable run of hits well into the 1980s.

Although they'd only release one further single in 1960 *(Man Of Mystery)* to re-enter the UK Top 10, The Shadows would really start stepping out in February 1961, when *FBI* would become their third Top 10 single and only the first of four to achieve the feat that year - *Frightened City,* the No. 1 *Kon-Tiki,* and *The Savage* being the others.

All in all, The Shadows would score three more No. 1 hits down the years (*Wonderful Land* and *Dance On* in 1962, and *Foot Tapper* in 1963) and a staggering 18 Top 10 hits in all before officially calling it a day as a full-time unit in 1981.

In the meanwhile, The Shadows had stamped their mark on a generation of international record-buyers, with Hank Marvin due special credit for inspiring a generation of guitar players. Bruce Welch (along with bassist John Rostill, who joined in 1963) would also direct and produce all of the early hits which made Olivia Newton-John a star.

Sadly, The Shadows would share Cliff Richard's inability to persuade US pop fans to take him to their hearts, and the version of *Apache* which would become a huge hit in America, was the cover version by a Danish guitarist, Jorgen Ingmann.

ALL CHANGE MEANS NO CHANGE FOR EVERLYS

News that The Everly Brothers, Don and Phil, had signed with the newly-formed Warner Bros. record company at the end of 1959 raised all kinds of questions.

Did this mean they'd forsake the Nashville country sound which had made them one of the most distinctive and consistently successful acts of the late 1950s? Would a West Coast-based operation with no proven track record be able to tap into the vast reservoir of good will the brothers had created over the past three years?

The answers were a qualified 'yes' and an unqualified 'certainly', as the immediate outstanding success of The Everly Brothers' first Warners single, *Cathy's Clown,* proved. The sound was bigger and tougher, but it was to become their biggest international hit since the 1958 smash *All I Have To Do Is Dream.*

In fact, the transition would be achieved effortlessly as the duo's former record company helped by continuing to release 'old' Everly Brothers material (*Let It Be Me, When Will I Be Loved* and *Like Strangers*) in 1960, while Warners would help the boys score with the newly-recorded double A-sided *Lucille/So Sad (To Watch Good Love Go Bad)*.

It's now clear that Don and Phil continued to use the same Nashville studios and musicians. All that changed was the fact that they now had artistic control and could start recording songs they felt better reflected them and the changing times.

MISS DYNAMITE EXPLODES TO STARDOM

A phenomenon in US country music circles since the age of 13, this year saw the international breakthrough of the now 16-year-old Brenda Lee with the first hits in what would prove enough to help her rival Connie Francis as the most influential female pop voice of the early 1960s.

Already a US hit in 1959, *Sweet Nothin's* would provide the tiny girl with the big, explosive voice (hence her nickname, 'Little Miss Dynamite') with her first British and European hit and the launching pad she needed to build that formidable track record.

By the end of the year, Brenda (born Brenda Mae Tarpley) would score with *I'm Sorry* and *I Want To Be Wanted*, while 1961 would see her enjoy big international hits with *Let's Jump The Broomstick*, *Emotions*, *Dum Dum* and *Fool No 1*.

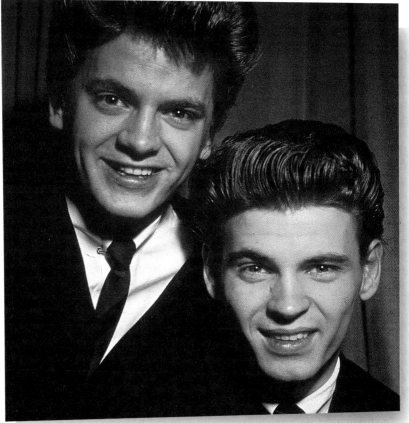

The Everly Brothers

SEPT

SEPTEMBER 26

Nixon And Kennedy Lock Horns In TV Debate

REFLECTING THE HOPEFULNESS and innovation which inevitably came with a new decade, American presidential candidates Richard M. Nixon and John F. Kennedy set new standards for democratic discussion today when they appeared together in the world's first ever nationally televised debate.

The combatants ended with a handshake after an hour which seemed - to most commentators - to prove that there were relatively few topics on which they disagreed greatly. The general feeling among viewers polled for their opinions seemed to be that what had been said made little, if any, difference to the way they had already decided to vote.

Nixon, the current Republican Vice-President, accused his Democrat opponent of reckless public spending policies which could only be paid for by taxpayers. Kennedy responded by complaining that Nixon was heartless in his failure to support the rise in the statutory minimum wage to $1 per hour, his refusal to provide State medical care for the elderly and his lack of interest in expanding the programme for building more schools.

The result? An honourable tie.

SEPTEMBER 12

Ulbricht Becomes East German Supremo

The East German regime consolidated the power and unrivalled supremacy of the Communist Party today when it announced the abolition of the post of President, choosing to create the title Head of State for Walther Ulbricht, its Stalinist leader since 1946.

The move, which followed East Germany's worrying closure of the East-West border in Berlin last month, was taken as another sign that the East German authorities had closed the door firmly on any slim chances there may have been of further talks to attempt the reunification of a country divided since 1945.

Whatever Next? London Gets First Moving Pavement

City of London tube commuters got their first taste of futuristic foot transportation today when the first travelator became operational at Bank station for the first time.

An American invention, the travelator worked on a similar mechanical principle to the escalator but, instead of raising or lowering passengers to a different level, moved along the ground like a mobile pavement.

Installed to help passengers changing lines, and providing a connecting link between the Northern and Central Lines on the one hand, and the District and Circle Lines on the other, the travelator gave commuters access from Bank station to Monument station (a distance of several hundred yards) without having to ascend to street level.

In later years, of course, travelators would become a familiar feature of many large airports. Right now, they were science fiction come true.

Congo Tragedy Turns To Take-Over Farce

The bloodstained birth of the independent Congo turned to tragic farce this month as opposing forces tried to use the chaos of civil war to stake their own claims to power.

The first move came on September 5, when a weary President Kasavubu fired his troublesome Prime Minister, Patrice Lumumba. The latter refused to step down, announcing that he was sacking the President instead, beginning a sorry exchange of threats and pronouncements which did nothing to clarify the situation.

On September 9, Lumumba made his most daring strategic move when, in defiance of UN commanders' advice and orders, he ordered his forces into the breakaway province of Katanga. President Kasavubu's response was to fire Lumumba again, pronouncing Joseph Ileo the new premier.

Ileo's period in office would last a mere five days. On September 14, the head of the Congolese Army, Colonel Joseph Désiré Mobutu, strode into a bar in the capital, Lopoldville, and told confused foreign journalists that he'd taken over. President Kasavubu and his new Prime Minister had both been dismissed, Patrice Lumumba had been arrested, and he'd ordered parliament to be suspended.

The next day, Mobutu would begin making his own appointments and, on September 20, the Congo would have its third government in as many months.

SEPTEMBER 23

Khrushchev Rattles UN Cage As Cold War Hots Up

DETERMINED TO MAKE HIS VISIT to the UN headquarters in New York memorable, Soviet leader Nikita Khrushchev used his speech to the General Assembly today to rattle a few cages.

Hot on the heels of the abandoned Paris summit, when he'd used the capture of U-2 spy-plane pilot Gary Powers to force President Eisenhower into an impossible corner, and the inevitable cancellation of Eisenhower's planned visit to Moscow, Khrushchev went for the jugular by demanding that Dag Hammarskjöld be fired from his job as the UN's Secretary-General, and that the organization's headquarters be located somewhere other than in the United States.

While the heated discussions these demands created rumbled on, Khrushchev worked his way into the spotlight again on September 29 by heckling and banging on a table during a speech by British Prime Minister Harold Macmillan. Relations between countries on opposite sides of the Iron Curtain appeared to have reached an all-time low.

As Khrushchev's antics in October would prove, they still had further depths to plumb.

SEPTEMBER 19

Traffic Wardens Go Ticket-Happy

The day London's drivers had long dreaded - the arrival of traffic wardens with powers to impose fines on those breaking parking regulations - was every bit as horrid as they'd thought.

To no one's surprise, and to the dismay of those 'hit' by the new enemy, almost 350 parking ticket fines were stuck on offending cars' windscreens between 9 am and 6.30 pm today. What next? The thought police?

Shads To Quit Cliff?

With their début single *Apache* lodged firmly at No. 1 in the British charts all this month, The Shadows - teen idol Cliff Richard's backing group - announced plans to tour the country on their own.

As rumours spread that they intended to go it alone full-time, the quartet - Hank Marvin, Brian Bennett, Jet Harris and Tony Meehan - were forced to issue a statement saying the move was only a temporary split. They'd be doing their nifty steps (now made into a dance craze by British teens and copied by every three-guitars-and-drums group in the land) behind Cliff for some time yet.

SEPTEMBER 16

Speed Ace Campbell's Miracle Escape

British speed king Donald Campbell, son of the pioneering land- and water-speed record holder, Sir Malcolm Campbell, miraculously survived a crash in his latest *Bluebird* - the name given to all Campbell vehicles - which destroyed the car during trials at Bonneville Salt Flats in Utah today.

Campbell's escape was all the more remarkable considering that *Bluebird* was travelling at 350 mph at the time. His father's land speed record, achieved at the same site in 1935, still stood at 301.129 mph, so the young daredevil knew he had it beaten, as long as he could keep his car in one piece!

Water, Water, Everywhere

Within three days this month, areas of two different continents were devastated by floods, each experiencing similar initial problems, but only one facing almost insurmountable long-term obstacles to full recovery.

On October 9, heavy rainstorms, high tides and storm-force winds combined to hit southern England with the worst flood disaster since 1953. Given modern reclamation methods and equipment, it would only be a matter of time before things returned more or less to normality.

Which is more than can be said for the unfortunate people of East Pakistan who, on October 11, were dealt the double blow of being swamped by a tidal wave as well as hit by a hurricane. One of the world's most impoverished and overcrowded nations, East Pakistan reported thousands of deaths in the devastation which followed.

For them, and the survivors who literally had to pick up the pieces, normality would never return.

Nigeria Gains Its Independence **OCTOBER 1**

In keeping with time-honoured tradition, the former British West African colony of Nigeria achieved its independence, and became the continent's most populous State, at the stroke of midnight last night. Retaining its links with Britain as a member of the Commonwealth, Nigeria had grown through almost 60 years of colonial status into a nation of 35 million inhabitants with a potential for economic strength founded on its large oil reserves and its success as an international trading centre.

In contrast to the outburst delivered a few months earlier by Patrice Lumumba when the Congo achieved independence, Prime Minister Tafawa Balewa spoke of the 'affection and loyalty' Nigerians felt for Britain and for Princess Alexandra, who represented the Queen at independence celebrations.

OCTOBER 12

Doin' The Khrushchev Stomp!

AFTER HIS FUN AND GAMES in the UN General Assembly last month, heckling and abusing Harold Macmillan and UN Secretary-General Hammarskjöld, Russia's Nikita Khrushchev continued his one-man UN disruption campaign today when he used one of his shoes to emphasize his bellicose point of view.

Khrushchev's cabaret came this time during a speech by a delegate from the Philippines, who claimed that the Soviet Union was guilty of imperialistic behaviour in Eastern Europe. Quickly removing one of his shoes, the Russian leader banged it on the table in front of him as he described his accuser as 'this jerk, this American stooge'.

The Khrushchev brogue (definitely not a mass-produced Russian item, as sold - when available - in Moscow's GUM department store) was waved again during a speech by the US Assistant Secretary of State, Francis Wilcox. But it was the refusal of the Romanian Foreign Minister to give way which forced Assembly President Boland to use his gavel to end what had been a remarkably rowdy session of the world's peace-keeping body.

The American sense of humour and search for profit being what they are, a tape copy was made of the noise produced by Khrushchev's banging, and used as the basis for a novelty record titled *The Khrushchev Stomp*. Sadly, this little gem made no impact on the US pop charts…

Japan In Turmoil As MP Is Assassinated

The political shock waves which ran through Japan today probably registered on seismic equipment thousands of miles away. They followed the public murder of a prominent socialist member of parliament at a political rally.

Part of the revulsion was due to the manner in which Inejiro Asanuma died - run through with a traditional sword wielded in samurai warrior fashion by a fanatical right-wing student. In the two days of protests which followed Asanuma's murder, a number of student organization offices were ransacked and their occupants attacked.

UK TOP 10 SINGLES

1: Only The Lonely
- Roy Orbison
2: Tell Laura I Love Her
- Ricky Valance
3: As Long As He Needs Me
- Shirley Bassey
4: How About That
- Adam Faith
5: Nine Times Out Of Ten
- Cliff Richard
6: So Sad (To Watch Good Love Go Bad)
- The Everly Brothers
7: Walk Don't Run
- The John Barry Seven
8: Apache
- The Shadows
9: Chain Gang
- Sam Cooke
10: Let's Think About Living
- Bob Luman

Born this month:
5: Careca, Brazilian international soccer star
6: Richard Jobson, UK rock singer (The Skids), TV presenter, style guru
13: Joey Belladonna, US rock singer, songwriter (Anthrax)
14: Steve Cram, UK athlete; British, European, Commonwealth and World 800m and 1500m champion, Olympic silver medallist
19: Daniel 'Woody' Woodgate, UK pop musician (Madness)
30: Diego Maradona, Argentinian international soccer star *(see Came & Went pages)*

OCTOBER 3

Labour Split As Gaitskell Loses Disarmament Debate

A MAJOR POLICY CONFLICT over the question of nuclear disarmament caused a huge rift in the British Labour Party today as one of its leading lights resigned, apparently as a consequence of the leadership's apparent unwillingness to listen to the party's rank and file.

Close to tears at times, party leader Hugh Gaitskell (pictured) tried, with all his considerable command of emotional oratory, to convince the Labour Party Conference that it was unrealistic for Britain to try to go it alone and abandon its nuclear deterrent. But the growing tide of left-wing disarmers rejected his objections and voted for unilateral nuclear disarmament to become Labour Party policy.

With his enemies baying for his blood, it was a measure of Gaitskell's political skills that he managed to beat off a leadership challenge mounted by Harold Wilson, an original member of the left-wing Bevanite faction, only three weeks later.

The day before the crucial vote, the party was rocked by the resignation from its National Executive Committee of Anthony Wedgwood Benn, whose energetic arguments for nuclear disarmament had added to Labour's air of disunity. The ranks of the Labour Left would be increased on November 18 when Michael Foot won the Ebbw Vale seat of the late Nye Bevan.

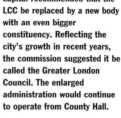

London To Get New Government?

For many years, Britain's capital had its local government affairs overseen by the LCC, the London County Council, from its massive County Hall building which stands on the River Thames, almost opposite the Houses of Parliament.

All that seemed likely to change today, when a Royal Commission report on the capital recommended that the LCC be replaced by a new body with an even bigger constituency. Reflecting the city's growth in recent years, the commission suggested it be called the Greater London Council. The enlarged administration would continue to operate from County Hall.

British Pop Fans Vote Elvis And Connie The Tops

Everyone likes popularity polls, even if it's only to disagree with the results! Now the most influential international trawl of what teenagers really go for, Britain's *New Musical Express* Readers' Poll this month confirmed that two years away from the scene with the US Army had done nothing to shake the loyalty of the thousands of fans who voted Elvis Presley the world's top male singer.

Strangely, though his age and image ought to have put him out of the reckoning with a readership steeped in rock 'n' roll, veteran crooner Frank Sinatra still managed to rate a third position in that section, just behind Britain's Cliff Richard, who - naturally - also won the British male singer section.

Connie Francis held on to the international female singer title she won last year, but found herself hard-pressed by newcomer Brenda Lee and a third-placed Shirley Bassey, who pipped the British section over Alma Cogan and Petula Clark. Best group of 1960? The Shadows, of course, who also won the Disc of the Year award with *Apache.*

OCTOBER 30
DIEGO MARADONA - THE TORMENTED GENIUS

As the first man since the legendary Pelé to be generally recognized as the world's greatest soccer player, Diego Maradona - who was born today in the Buenos Aires district of Lanus - is likely to go down in history for the failings which proved him to be a mere mortal, and an often deeply flawed one, at that.

A professional with Argentinos Júniors from the age of 15 and an international player at just 16, Maradona was only 22 when Spanish champions Barcelona paid £4.8 million for his services. His value was reckoned to be £6.9 million only two years later when Napoli persuaded him to move to Italy.

If that seemed a lot to critics of escalating transfer fees, Napoli had excellent return for their outlay when Maradona's midfield genius and goal-scoring abilities contributed hugely to their 1987 Italian League and Cup double, the UEFA Cup win in 1989 and the Italian League title win in 1990.

It's impossible to estimate his value to the Argentinian national team, and while all the film and photographic evidence later proved that he had, as England goalkeeper Peter Shilton alleged, handled the ball to score one of the goals which put Argentina into the 1986 World Cup Final, his complete command of a full range of dazzling skills left opponents and commentators lost for adequate words of praise.

Off the pitch, Maradona's life was spinning out of control, and his arrest - in 1991, for possession of cocaine - led to tabloid revelations of heavy drinking, women and criminal associations. Ordered to undertake a rehabilitation programme by an Argentinian court (he'd been suspended by Napoli), Maradona was still, at the age of 32, considered worth £4.48 million to the Spanish club, Sevilla, though his continued personal waywardness made that a bad investment.

Recalled triumphantly to the Argentina national team for the 1994 World Cup in the United States, Maradona was tested positive for illegal performance-enhancing drugs.

Back in Argentina, he tried to move into management but again fell foul of the authorities with increasingly bizarre behaviour, including the firing of airgun shots at journalists camped outside his home. It appeared to spell the sad end for the man who set and broke innumerable records at club and international level and who was, at his peak, completely unique.

JULY 6
NYE BEVAN - THE WORKERS' CHAMPION

More than perhaps any other single figure, Aneurin Bevan, who died today at the age of 63, represented the traditional face of Britain's Labour Party as the political arm of the nation's working class. Chief architect of the National Health Service, Bevan never lost sight of the grinding poverty and inequalities he'd witnessed as a young man and which he fought all his life to eliminate.

Known universally as 'Nye', Bevan followed his Welsh father into the mines at the age of 13 and rose through the trade union movement to become the South Wales miners' spokesman in the 1926 General Strike. The Member of Parliament for Ebbw Vale from 1929 until his death, he was Churchill's most constructive critic during the war, and became Minister of Health in

1945 when Labour swept to power.

Enraged by the imposition of NHS prescription charges to help meet defence costs in 1951, he resigned from the cabinet, forming what was called the 'Bevanite Left' to fight subsequent Labour support for nuclear arms. Chief Labour foreign affairs spokesman during the Suez crisis, he had been appointed the party's deputy leader in 1959, although it was known that he was suffering from the cancer which killed him.

Clark Gable

NOVEMBER 16
CLARK GABLE - THE RELUCTANT HEART-THROB

There's little doubt that the strain of filming *The Misfits*, in often impossible desert heat at a time when he was ill contributed hugely to the heart attack which killed Clark Gable today. But it's not likely he would have blamed anyone but himself. He was a pro, and that's what pros had to do to qualify for the title.

For 30 years one of Hollywood's most popular players – and for many years amused and bemused by the fact that, despite his large ears and what he described as a 'limited' dramatic range, millions of women considered him very sexy – Gable was a class act.

After a stint on Broadway, Gable made his film début in 1930 and quickly established himself as a gifted and witty actor, especially if he was given a feisty female protagonist like Joan Crawford (with whom he had a much-publicized affair in 1932 when they made *Possessed*), Jean Harlow or Claudette Colbert, his co-star in the 1934 classic *It Happened One Night*, for which he won his only Academy Award.

Likely to be remembered most for his devilishly smooth Rhett Butler in *Gone With The Wind*, Clark Gable was a one-off whose death was a severe loss to the screen-acting profession.

NOVEMBER 9

JFK First Past The Post - But Only Just!

JOHN FITZGERALD KENNEDY became the new President of the United States today, but the Democratic candidate's victory over his Republican opponent, the former Vice-President, Richard Nixon, was achieved by the incredibly small margin of little more than 100,000 votes - 'a nose' in horse-racing terms.

The final outcome was so close that Nixon refused to concede defeat until the day after the election, his tearful wife, Patricia, beside him.

Aged only 43, Kennedy became the youngest ever President of the United States, and also the first Roman Catholic to hold America's highest public office.

In contrast to the tearful scenes at Nixon's campaign HQ in Los Angeles, Kennedy's confirmation of his close-run triumph was made to excited and elated Democratic Party workers at the Cape Cod Armory, Hyannis, Massachusetts, his home turf. His pregnant wife Jacqueline beside him on the platform, Kennedy announced with a broad grin, 'So now my wife and I prepare for a new administration, and a new baby!'

The new President was no stranger to the corridors of power and privilege. His father, Joseph Kennedy, was a self-made Irish-American millionaire who'd served as US Ambassador in London during WWII, and made the Democratic Party in Massachusetts his personal fiefdom.

His son was educated at two of America's most famous

colleges, Princeton and Harvard, and many of his advisers were the contemporary products of Ivy League seats of learning. They represented the complete opposite of the departing Eisenhower's think-tank, which comprised conservative representatives from the world of business and industry, and they were more than ready to help JFK steer the United States across his 'new frontier'.

US Nuclear Subs To Use British Base

British Prime Minister Harold Macmillan fired the starting gun on what would prove an acrimonious and lengthy row today when he announced a government bill to allow US nuclear submarines to use the Holy Loch naval base in Scotland.

Although correctly confident that the Conservatives' parliamentary majority would be enough to see the bill become law, Macmillan also knew the decision was highly controversial, giving his opponents on all sides of the political spectrum many sticks with which to beat him - the anti-nuclear lobby, local residents and those who'd consider a US sub base a further surrender of sovereignty, included.

New Elvis Album Answers Religious Critics

Long the subject of vilification by fundamentalist preachers who believed his on-stage gyrations and raunchy songs made him the Devil's helpmate, rock superstar Elvis Presley tried to prove that he was a God-fearing, good ole Southern Baptist boy when he released an album of religious songs this month. Titled His *Hand In Mine*, it consisted of hymns and other sacred material The King said had always been important to him and his late and much-lamented mother, Gladys.

Benn Begins Battle To Be Mister

Left-wing Labour Party rebel MP Anthony Wedgwood Benn today embarked on what would be a three-year fight to stay an ordinary 'Mister' when he tried to renounce the title he'd just inherited on the death of his father, Viscount Stansgate. As a lord he couldn't stay in the House of Commons, and he didn't want to continue his political life among the dusty decrepitude of the House of Lords.

When his renunciation was rejected, Benn defied the system (not for the last time) by running in the by-election his peerage caused, doubling his majority. Refused permission to take his seat - he was still a noble, regardless of what the voters of Bristol wanted - it would not be until August 1963 that good sense and justice prevailed and plain old Mr Tony Benn returned to a seat in the Commons to do his own inimitable thing.

UK TOP 10 SINGLES

1: It's Now Or Never
- Elvis Presley
2: As Long As He Needs Me
- Shirley Bassey
3: Dreamin'
- Johnny Burnette
4: Only The Lonely
- Roy Orbison
5: Rocking Goose
- Johnny & The Hurricanes
6: My Heart Has A Mind Of Its Own
- Connie Francis
7: Save The Last Dance For Me
- The Drifters
8: Let's Think About Living
- Bob Luman
9: Goodness Gracious Me
- Peter Sellers and Sophia Loren
10: My Love For You
- Johnny Mathis

Gilbert Harding, TV Superstar, Dies

NOVEMBER 16

Britain lost its first true TV superstar today when Gilbert Harding (pictured far right), the rough, gruff and irascible star of BBC's panel show *What's My Line?,* collapsed and died of a heart attack on the steps of the corporation's radio HQ, Broadcasting House, in London.

The son of parents who ran a workhouse, the 53-year-old Harding had been a teacher after graduating from Cambridge University, became a policeman for a while, but joined the BBC during WWII. A regular on such radio hits as *Round Britain Quiz, The Brains Trust* and *Twenty Questions,* he'd joined *What's My Line?* in 1951 when BBC TV first brought the American show to British screens.

Harding's obvious inability to suffer fools made his appearances on *What's My Line?* unmissable, and led to him having to make on-air apologies for his rudeness. His fall came out of the blue in September this year when he broke down in tears during the gruelling warts-and-all interview show *Face To Face,* when host John Freeman pushed him for details about his relationship with his mother.

A closet homosexual and alcoholic, Harding was unable to cope with the mass-media coverage his tears created and hit the bottle with a vengeance. His death allowed the scandal floodgates to open (the dead can't sue), and British tabloid readers were able to read the truth about the man they'd loved to hate.

Congolese And UN Troops In Gun Battle

In the most serious confrontation yet in the Congo, Tunisian troops of the UN peace-keeping force found themselves coming under cannon and machine-gun fire from the Congolese Army today as they and Ghanaian Embassy police stopped the arrest and deportation of the Ambassador of Ghana, Nathaniel Welbeck.

Seven Tunisians were reported killed in the battle, which also claimed the lives of a Congolese colonel and five soldiers.

Confrontation became inevitable when the Congolese accused Mr Welbeck of plotting to bring back Patrice Lumumba, the Congo Prime Minister deposed by army leader Colonel Mobutu. Defying an order to leave the country, the Ambassador had barricaded himself in his official residence, and warning shots from the UN force were met with a bombardment by approaching Congolese troops.

Sun Sets On Movie Legends

This month saw the world entertainment industry mourning the loss of two Hollywood celebrities. Pioneering silent film director Mack Sennett, creator and director of the riotous and classic Keystone Cops comedies, died at the age of 80, on November 5. The man who made stars of people like Charlie Chaplin and Chester Conklin made few films after the introduction of sound, but his outstanding contribution to screen comedy was recognized in 1937 when he was given a special Academy Award. November 16 saw the shock death of matinée idol Clark Gable, just two months short of his sixtieth birthday. Most famous for his memorable portrayal of Rhett Butler in the 1940 screen classic *Gone With The Wind,* Gable had first become obviously ill during the filming of *The Misfits,* in which he co-starred with Marilyn Monroe and Montgomery Clift. *(See Came & Went pages for a full appreciation)*

Official: Wives And Servants Can Read 'Lady C'

THE USUALLY SEDATE, solemn and hushed atmosphere of London's Old Bailey courtroom was disturbed by applause and cheers today when a jury decided that *Lady Chatterley's Lover* - D.H. Lawrence's notorious and long-banned novel which told of the relationship between a nobleman's wife, whose war-wounded husband was incapable of satisfying her sexual needs, and the gamekeeper who was, and did - was suitable for general consumption in an unexpurgated form.

The test case had been brought against Penguin Books, who'd admitted that an uncut version of the book had been printed in anticipation of the jury's favourable decision. Their defence claimed that while Lady Chatterley did contain titillating language and frank descriptions of various sexual encounters, the novel was serious and seriously artistic. Numerous critics and leading literary figures testified on behalf of Penguin.

The trial, which began on October 20 with extensive press and TV coverage of the trial - including Griffith-Jones's listing of 13 bouts of sexual intercourse 'with the emphasis always on the pleasure, the satisfaction, the sensuality' and his itemizing of the 30 occasions a certain Anglo-Saxon word appeared - only served to provide Penguin Books with an unprecedented free marketing campaign.

When the first print-run of 200,000 copies of *Lady Chatterley's Lover* went on sale in Britain on November 10 - costing 3/6 (18p) - every single one was sold.

DEC

Congo Crisis Deepens As Lumumba Is Arrested

THE ALREADY VOLATILE CONGO CRISIS deepened today when a three-day manhunt for deposed Prime Minister Patrice Lumumba (pictured) - who'd escaped from house arrest in Léopoldville - ended with his arrest *en route* to Stanleyville, where he was to join rebel forces loyal to him.

Enraged by the news, Lumumba's troops rounded up more than 1,000 European men, women and children and began beating and whipping them in retaliation. A number of United Nations officials were present to observe and report the violence, but were unable to prevent it.

His hands tied behind his back, Lumumba was flown the 400 miles back to the capital and driven, with a group of his aides, to the more secure surroundings of a military barracks. The government of Colonel Mobutu announced that he would face trial, charged with inciting the army to mutiny.

Lumumba would never be allowed to defend himself in court. In February 1961 his death - allegedly at the hands of villagers who found him and two companions in the bush, on the run again - would be announced. Patrice Lumumba was said to have been buried immediately, where he died.

Zulu Chief Luthuli Wins Peace Prize

Never afraid to court controversy, the Nobel Peace Prize committee outraged white South African opinion today when it awarded this year's coveted honour to Albert Luthuli, a Zulu chief deposed by the South African Government in 1956, charged with high treason for his leadership of the anti-apartheid African National Congress, and sentenced to exile on a remote farm.

Forbidden to travel, he would not collect his Peace Prize in Oslo, nor be able to take his seat when Glasgow University students elected him Rector, an honorary post intended to pay tribute to its recipient.

Strictly opposed to violence in his people's fight for freedom, Luthuli would die in 1967, supposedly falling in front of a railway train.

Leigh Divorces Sir Larry

Less than three weeks after the death of Clark Gable, her co-star in the classic movie version of *Gone With The Wind*, British actress Vivien Leigh - a timeless Scarlett O'Hara to Gable's immortal Rhett Butler - was granted a divorce from her real-life partner, Sir Laurence Olivier. The high society toasts of two continents and the London theatre world in their romantic heyday, Leigh and Larry were known to have drifted apart some time ago. The once beautiful actress had suffered a number of nervous breakdowns, and Sir Laurence was known to believe her illnesses were due as much to hysteria as they were to real psychological problems.

Belgians Boring? Don't Believe It!

Often characterized by outsiders as rather dull and uninspiring, the Belgians proved they could be just as volatile as the next hothead this month, and wild enough to bring their ruler's honeymoon to a premature conclusion.

Only two weeks after his wedding was the cause of national celebrations, King Baudouin of Belgium was heading back to Brussels today with his new queen, the Spanish-born Dona Fabiola de Moran y Aragon, to try to restore calm after nationwide unrest.

That began as routine protests against government cost-cutting measures, but exploded into violence when a heated parliamentary debate degenerated into a fist-fight on December 23. Nicely ignoring things like holiday spirit, good will to men and all that stuff, trouble increased and spread until the newly-weds were forced to come home.

UK TOP 10 SINGLES

1: It's Now Or Never
- Elvis Presley
2: Save The Last Dance For Me
- The Drifters
3: I Love You
- Cliff Richard
4: Strawberry Fair
- Anthony Newley
5: Goodness Gracious Me
- Peter Sellers and Sophia Loren
6: Little Donkey
- Nina and Frederick
7: Rocking Goose
- Johnny & The Hurricanes
8: Man Of Mystery
- The Shadows
9: Poetry In Motion
- Johnny Tillotson
10: Lonely Pup (In A Christmas Shop)
- Adam Faith

DECEMBER 5

Leyland To Buy Standard-Triumph

The ownership of British family car-manufacturing companies began to resemble a one-horse race today when Leyland Motors announced it was to take over the historic Standard-Triumph International, makers of the staid Standard saloons and the more racy Triumph sports cars.

With Leyland already boasting the Austin and Morris companies under its umbrella, their expanded operation would far outpace the US-owned Ford Motor Company's British output.

DECEMBER 13

123 Killed As Algerian Riots Greet De Gaulle

PRESIDENT CHARLES DE GAULLE (pictured) returned to Paris tonight, his face reflecting the knowledge that his five-day tour of Algeria had resulted in the deaths of 123 people in rioting by French settlers angered by the terms of the constitution he suggested to help the French colony win independence.

The President's repeated pledges to give the North African nation's Arab population full equality of rights and representation had been greeted with enthusiastic applause by members of that community. But they had further enraged an already furious French settler population and, more worryingly a large number of French Army officers and soldiers based in Algeria.

So, while huge crowds of Algerian Arabs greeted the general's progress with shouts of 'Vive de Gaulle!', his speeches triggered French extremist riots and the resulting deaths. President de Gaulle offered waiting press corps members no change of script as he arrived home.

'There is only one policy for Algeria,' he told them. 'Self-determination and reconciliation.' Neither appeared achievable in the immediate future.

DECEMBER 14

History Made As Test Ends In Tie

It had never happened before, and it's unlikely - thanks to the labyrinthine laws of cricket - to happen again. Today, in Brisbane, the first in a series of five five-day Test matches between Australia and the West Indies ended in a tie.

With Australia needing only six runs to win in the last over, with three batsmen available in case of the unimaginable, the unimaginable happened. Captain Ritchie Benaud was caught and Grout run out going for the winning run. The scores were level with two balls left when Lindsay Kline, the Australians' last man, came in. He pushed the first ball away and Meckiff, at the other end, came charging down the pitch intent on forcing the winning run.

Joe Solomon, who'd hurled the ball which ran out Grout only minutes earlier, repeated his feat and struck the stumps.

Last National Service Recruits Fall In

The last 2,049 men to be obliged to give two years of their young lives in the service of King (or Queen) and Country received their call-up papers today. They would bring to 5,300,000 the total of national servicemen enlisted since national conscription was introduced in 1939.

Of those who heeded the call today, 1,999 would join nine units of the British Army in the military garrison town of Aldershot for two weeks of basic training, while the others would elect to report to the RAF's Reception Centre at Cardington, Bedfordshire. Traditionally, very few

national servicemen chose to spend their two years in the Royal Navy.

With national service ended, the British armed forces would now have to rely on volunteer recruits, although a national neserve existed to boost numbers in the case of urgent need.

YOUR 1960 HOROSCOPE

Unlike most Western horoscope systems which group astrological signs into month-long periods based on the influence of 12 constellations, the Chinese believe that those born in the same year of their calendar share common qualities, traits and weaknesses with one of 12 animals - Rat, Ox, Tiger, Rabbit, Dragon, Snake, Horse, Sheep, Monkey, Rooster, Dog or Pig.

They also allocate the general attributes of five natural elements - Earth, Fire, Metal, Water, Wood - and an overall positive or negative aspect to each sign to summarize its qualities.

If you were born between February 8, 1959 and January 27, 1960, you are a Pig. As this book is devoted to the events of 1960, let's take a look at the sign which governs those born between January 28 that year and February 14, 1961 - The Year of The Rat

THE RAT
JANUARY 28, 1960 - FEBRUARY 14, 1961
ELEMENT: METAL ASPECT: (+)

Rats like to be pioneers, leaders of men and in the forefront of the action. As leaders they carry a somewhat majestic air, and they do well in any situation where they can be respected and admired. They are sociable, pleasant, amusing and born under the sign of charm.

Active, both physically and mentally, Rats tend to lead busy lives. They like a challenge, and to live dangerously, keeping their minds stimulated by having lots of projects always on the boil.

Rats are highly ambitious and are prepared to put a great deal of hard practical work in to achieve their objective - which they often do, being able to combine objectivity with imagination and perception. Sharply intuitive, Rats can see far ahead and go straight for their targets.

Best known for their charm, and possessors of a great sense of humour, Rats love to make an impact and leave a favourable impression. Home-loving and sensuous creatures, they can be extremely generous to the ones they love while being very frugal when it comes down to their basic living needs.

Rats are very loyal and renowned for standing by their loved ones. However, if they're confronted by real difficulties in life, they often find it hard to cope with the situation and become obsessive. Though considered tolerant and easy-going, there is always an implicit sense of anger and aggression which might break through.

Rat individuals generally control their feelings, presenting a cool front to the world even though they are very passionate. They find it hard to talk about their feelings, but do enjoy most forms of physical and sensual stimulation.

Rats are wiry and tenacious, and never give up easily. They are considered lucky, and their broadminded approach to life makes them enjoy all kinds of new sensations and try to get as much out of life as they possibly can.

FAMOUS RATS

HM Queen Elizabeth The Queen Mother
HRH The Prince of Wales
HRH Prince Harry
HRH The Duke of York
Marlon Brando actor, Native American Rights campaigner
Doris Day actress, singer, dancer, businesswoman
Glenda Jackson Oscar-winning actress, now socialist politician
Sir Andrew Lloyd Webber composer, entrepreneur businessman
Gary Lineker international soccer star, TV presenter
Wayne Sleep modern dancer, choreographer, director
Yves St Laurent fashion designer, businessman